IMAGES
of America

LOWRY AIR
FORCE BASE

In 1944, Lowry Air Force Base held a design contest for a base insignia. Cpl. George Grimes won with this "Little Fellow" cartoon character. (Courtesy of Wings Over the Rockies Museum Photographic Archives.)

ON THE COVER: This September 25, 1948, photograph captured a B-36 heavy bomber aircraft flying low over Lowry Air Force Base's easily identified two huge hangars and flight line. (Courtesy of Wings Over the Rockies Museum Photographic Archives.)

IMAGES of America

LOWRY AIR FORCE BASE

Jack Stokes Ballard, John Bond,
and George Paxton

ARCADIA
PUBLISHING

Published by Arcadia Publishing
Charleston, South Carolina

Printed in the United States of America

Library of Congress Control Number: 2013930195

For all general information, please contact Arcadia Publishing:
Telephone 843-853-2070
Fax 843-853-0044
E-mail sales@arcadiapublishing.com
For customer service and orders:
Toll-Free 1-888-313-2665

Visit us on the Internet at www.arcadiapublishing.com

This book is dedicated to all those men and women, students and staff, military and civilian, who came to Lowry Air Force Base for expert instruction and then went on to serve our Air Force and our country, and to those who ably supported their education at this outstanding technical training center.

CONTENTS

FOREWORD

When I first arrived at Lowry Air Force Base to sign in at my new headquarters, I immediately began to understand and appreciate the outstanding contributions to our nation's security that Lowry had made during its long tenure as a military base. At that time, the flying mission had ceased, and Lowry was focused on training military and civilian men and women in technical areas so that they would be fully equipped to contribute to the national purpose. Often, the graduates of Lowry's training programs served as instructors at other bases, thus multiplying Lowry's impact. I found this to be significant.

Lowry AFB was established in the late 1930s. Its mission was to prepare military warriors from all branches of the US and Allied forces, and the base did just that for World War II, Korea, Vietnam, Gulf I, and many other incidents requiring military action in defending our country and ensuring its citizens' freedom. Over the years, Lowry changed to meet the demands of the times and was in the forefront of technology until it closed in 1994. Every man and woman, both military and civilian, who served at Lowry can be proud of their contributions to the nation.

Likewise, citizens of Colorado can be proud of the magnificent work of the Denver and Aurora city governments in developing and executing reuse plans for the 1,100 acres that Lowry AFB encompassed after closure. The Department of Defense used the Lowry closure and reuse success as a model for other base closures.

—Michael J. Wright
Colonel, USAF (Retired)
Lowry AFB's last commander

ACKNOWLEDGMENTS

The authors gratefully acknowledge the tremendous historical research, compilation, and writing about Lowry Air Force Base by Michael H. Levy and S.Sgt. Patrick M. Scanlan, who ably served as the training center historians. Their efforts, mainly documented in a published booklet entitled *Pursuit of Excellence: A History of Lowry Air Force Base, 1937–1987* (later supplemented with additional material, bringing the history to 1994), provide the broad foundation for this publication. Numerous volunteers interested in preserving the history of the base in photographs and articles, particularly beginning with the original Lowry Heritage Museum, made great contributions beyond the work of the center historians. One notable volunteer, John Bond, became the longtime compiler and administrator of the Wings Over the Rockies Air and Space Museum's photographic archives, which became the principal source of photographs for this book. The photographic archives are herein cited as WORMPA. Also greatly appreciated has been the support of director Greg Anderson, David Kerr, and other staff members of the Wings Over the Rockies Air and Space Museum.

INTRODUCTION

The Lowry Air Force Base motto, *Sustineo Alas* (I Sustain the Wings), adorned entryways of old base buildings. That inscription appropriately reflected the continuous mission of this Colorado air base from its inception in 1937: photography and armament training as the Denver branch of the Chanute (Illinois) Air Corps Technical School. During this 57-year span, until it closed in 1994, Lowry served as one of the nation's most important military technical training centers, providing the necessary skilled technicians, officers, and airmen to sustain Air Force operations through World War II, the Cold War, the Korean War, and the Vietnam War. Due to the urgent need for all types of trained personnel during World War II, the center operated three shifts, seven days a week, and sometimes 24 hours a day. Space was at a premium, and the Army Air Corps established a satellite school across town at Fort Logan to train clerical airmen. Lowry base population peaked at around 20,000 during World War II. After the war, the training included intensive instruction in armament (nuclear and conventional), avionics, electronics, fire protection and aircraft rescue, intelligence, supply, food service, clerical, ordnance disposal, and space systems operations. These wide-ranging training programs required the continuous updating of curriculum, staff expertise, and training equipment as technology rapidly advanced. By the 1980s, this effort involved a base population of 10,000 students, staff, and support personnel, providing a vital boost to the local economy.

While technical training remained the focus, Lowry also maintained air operations until 1966. In 1940, Lowry began training the first group of bombardier instructors, using the extensive bombing range to the southeast of the base. Over 100 aircraft occupied the ramps in 1945.

In 1955, Lowry AFB became the first location of the newly authorized Air Force Academy. The first class members arrived on July 11, and cadet training continued until August 1958, when the Colorado Springs site opened. Lowry AFB also hosted the Eisenhower Summer White House and filming of the movie *The Glenn Miller Story* in the 1950s.

As the missile and space age began, Lowry received new missions. Three Titan missile silos were emplaced on the old Lowry bombing range in October 1961, but they were deactivated in 1965. Space systems training involving both maintenance and operations began in the 1960s and involved classified work at satellite tracking installations at nearby Buckley Field.

Just as Lowry's emphasis on training and missions changed to missile and space technology, it became a victim of Department of Defense reorganizations, base closures, and economic pressures to consolidate training programs. As a consequence, Lowry Air Force Base closed on September 30, 1994. It could reflect on its history and proudly proclaim that its 1.1 million skilled graduates had indeed sustained (*Sustineo Alas*) the nation's wings.

One

THE BEGINNING
1937

Lowry Field, later to become Lowry Air Force Base, came into existence at the present location in March 1938. The Lowry name and the enthusiasm for flying, however, dated to 1924, when the Colorado National Guard named the airport at Thirty-eighth Avenue and Dahlia Street, east of Denver's present-day Park Hill Golf Course, Lowry Field.

Lt. Francis B. Lowry, a Denver resident, was killed in 1918 in France while serving as an artillery observer and aerial photographer for the Army Air Service. Lieutenant Lowry rests in the Fairmount Cemetery near the base, and the field and base were named for him.

The grounds and original facilities were occupied by the Agnes Phipps Memorial Sanatorium. Lawrence C. Phipps built the medical facility east of Denver in 1903 for the treatment of tuberculosis during the era of fresh air care. It had closed and been vacant for six years.

In 1934, the Army found it necessary to relocate the photography and armament schools from Chanute Field in Illinois. A search began for a new site. The citizens of Denver, seeing the economic advantages of having a military establishment, bought the sanatorium land and buildings and offered them to the Army. On August 27, 1937, Pres. Franklin D. Roosevelt signed legislation authorizing funds for the Army's training at Denver.

On October 1, 1937, Capt. Harold D. Stetson raised the American flag over the Phipps Sanatorium, establishing the Denver branch of the Air Corps Training School located at Chanute Field. The remodeled sanatorium buildings became the administration and classroom facilities.

New students arrived in February 1938, and the year proved to be a busy one for the new training center. Lt. Col. Junius W. Jones became the first commanding officer, and instruction in aerial photography and armament began that month. The planes from the old Lowry Field were transferred to Denver Municipal Airport, and hangars were dismantled, moved, and reassembled at the new base. The name "Lowry" was officially assigned to the new Air Corps site on March 21, 1938. In June, nine aircraft were ferried from the Denver Municipal Airport (later to be renamed in honor of Mayor Ben Stapleton). A four-year, $3.5-million program of new construction got underway. In October, instruction expanded to include a clerical school.

The new Lowry Field continued to grow, from 1,400 personnel in December 1939 to 8,000 in June 1941. As the international situation deteriorated, the number of classes increased significantly, all in preparation for the challenges to come in the World War II years.

This Denver-area airport, located at Thirty-eighth Avenue and Dahlia Street northeast of the city, was used by the Colorado National Guard beginning in 1923. It was called Lowry Field in 1924, named after World War I aerial observer Lt. Francis B. Lowry. In this early photograph, note the military tents and "Lowry Field" spelled out on top of the hangar.

In 1923, the 120th Observation Squadron (Eyes of the Army), 45th Division Air Service, Colorado National Guard, was mustered into state service. This close-up view of the National Guard hangars and Douglas 0-38 aircraft at the 120th Observation Squadron's Lowry Field shows the facilities in the mid-1920s. The very first aircraft were the World War I Curtiss JN-4 "Jennies."

Following his historic flight from New York to Paris on May 20, 1927, Charles Lindbergh made a celebrated tour of the United States in the *Spirit of St. Louis*. He made 82 stops in all 48 states to promote the commercialization of aviation. On August 31, Lindbergh took off from Omaha, Nebraska, and after seven hours and 45 minutes landed at Lowry Field. After a day of celebration, he left on September 1 for Pierre, South Dakota.

Charles Lindbergh, accompanied by Colorado governor Billy Adams (to the left of Lindbergh in the rear seat) and Denver mayor Ben Stapleton (standing in the center of the car), starts out from Lowry Field on a city tour witnessed by hundreds of thousands of Denverites. During his visit, Lindbergh reportedly commented that Lowry Field was one of the finest equipped and maintained single-unit fields in the United States.

Lowry Field, and later Lowry Air Force Base, memorialized Lt. Francis B. Lowry, who was killed in World War I aerial combat on September 26, 1918. Lowry is shown here in a formal wartime photograph.

Lieutenant Lowry's remains were brought back to Denver, his hometown, in 1921 and given a hero's parade and burial. The funeral procession winds near Denver's Civic Center.

Lieutenant Lowry was buried and honored with this large monument at Fairmount Cemetery, which is near Lowry Air Force Base.

Phipps Sanatorium, built in 1903, was originally a tuberculosis treatment facility. It was chosen as the site for the Denver-area Army Air Corps training center. The vacant buildings were used initially to house administration offices and classrooms. As seen in this photograph, the patients' rooms had no front walls, as this was a part of the fresh air treatment prevalent at the time of the sanatorium's operation.

In September 1937, Capt. Harold D. Stetson was transferred from Fort Logan to the airfield. On October 1, the flag was raised for the first time at the new Lowry base. Captain Stetson, an engineer, assumed command, and by October 4, construction began on the site's conversion.

LOWRY'S FIRST COMMANDER
CAPTAIN HAROLD D. STETSON

Lowry Air Force Base would begin as the Denver Branch of the Air Corps Training School at Chanute Field, Illinois. On February 26, 1938, officers were introduced to the public at a luncheon given at the new airfield by the Denver Chamber of Commerce.

Lt. Col. Junius W. Jones, in uniform, became commander of Lowry. In this February 1938 photograph, he is shown with Denver mayor Ben Stapleton (second from right) and Charles A. Shinn, president of the Denver Chamber of Commerce. The lady and child are not identified.

Shortly after the location of the Army Air Corps Training Center was determined, the first cadre of personnel arrived in Denver in February 1938. Men offloaded from train cars into waiting buses.

An Army construction crew and cars struggle with the mud, marking the scene of early Lowry development. The large structure under construction is Building 349.

The Colorado National Guard's 120th Observation Squadron began its move to the new Army Air Corps Lowry Field, disassembling its hangars and reconstructing them not far from the Phipps Sanatorium.

This photograph, looking southeast, was taken very early in the conversion of the former sanatorium to the new Lowry Field. The old hangars from the field at Thirty-eighth Avenue and Dahlia and the foundation of Hangar No. 1 are in the background. Officers' housing are visible in the foreground. The intersection in the foreground is Sixth Avenue and Quebec Street.

A huge hangar, Building 402, is shown under construction in April 1939. It would be 300 feet long and 290 feet wide, with a ceiling nearly 90 feet above the ground. Begun in August 1938, it would be completed in August 1939 and become Hangar No. 1.

This aerial view of Lowry Field in December 1938 centers on the Phipps Sanatorium, but in the upper portion of the photograph, the old National Guard hangars at the original Lowry Field have been reassembled, and the beginning of Hangar No. 1 can be seen in the upper right.

The nearly completed Lowry Field Hangar No. 1 is captured in this mid-1939 photograph. "Lowry Field" can be seen spelled out on the roof.

Lowry Field construction progress can be seen in this 1939 photograph, with the outlines of runways appearing for the first time.

In the 1930s, this was nearby Denver Municipal Airport. The terminal is in the center. The field was small in the beginning but was destined to virtually overwhelm Lowry.

As Lowry Field continued to develop, Denver Municipal Airport likewise grew rapidly. This aerial view shows Denver Municipal to the north of Lowry, in the upper part of the photograph. The proximity of the two airfields would eventually become a serious problem.

This 1939 "General Mess" Christmas menu provides a glimpse of progress in the interior development of the base's buildings.

Two

AIR CORPS TECHNICAL SCHOOL
1937–1942

Colorado's blue sky, Western space, and a welcoming community were the factors that convinced the Army Air Corps to transfer its aerial photography school and armament training to Denver in 1937. Initially named the Denver Branch of the Air Corps Technical School (of Chanute Field), then named Lowry Field in 1938, both technical schools would become the main training centers for those specialties through World War II and after.

The beginnings were modest. Much of the credit for the development of the photography training school goes to M.Sgt. Grover B. Gilbert, a noncommissioned officer from Chanute Field who came to Lowry at the very beginning to establish the program. The first photography class consisted of 12 students. Classes were conducted for primary, secondary, and advanced levels. As demand increased, so did the response. In 1943, for example, 200 students arrived weekly. They specialized in photographic laboratory work, camera repair, cinematography, and production of training and orientation films for the Air Corps. Graduates went to war to take pictures from the air, much like Lieutenant Lowry did during World War I.

The armament school dealt with sidearms, machine guns, bombs, and bomb racks. As training intensified, land farther east of Lowry, called the Lowry Bombing Range, was acquired to allow for practice bombing runs. Urgently needed graduates were sent to armament sections of squadrons at air bases throughout the world.

The Lowry curriculum changed as technology evolved. When remote-control gun turrets were developed, Lowry became the only school to teach repair and maintenance of such turrets.

During World War II and after, Lowry developed relationships with companies such as General Electric (in the field of remote-control gunnery) and Kodak (for photography expertise). These relationships involved the exchange of both instructors and students. At the peak of World War II, Lowry also had a clerical school, located across town at Fort Logan, and armament classes at the auxiliary Buckley airfield to the east.

Aerial photography was extremely important at Lowry for the duration of the base's existence. This photograph captured the first class of a school for aerial photography in 1918 at Langley Field, Virginia.

AIR CORPS TECHNICAL SCHOOL
PHOTOGRAPHY --- CLASS NO. 1 -----------JULY 17, 1936
CHANUTE FIELD-----RANTOUL, ILLINOIS

Before the establishment of the photography school at Lowry, training took place at Chanute Field in Rantoul, Illinois. This July 17, 1936, photograph shows the Chanute technical school class No. 1, and an impressive array of cameras. M.Sgt. Grover B. Gilbert, third from left in the front row, was instrumental in scouting and establishing the Denver Branch of the Air Corps Technical School in late 1937. After a compromise was reached between Colorado and Illinois congressmen, the armament and photography school relocated to Denver, with men and equipment arriving on February 12, 1938.

Shown here is Lowry photography class No. 1 on April 15, 1938, in front of the Phipps Sanatorium building.

This 1940 photograph at Lowry shows students with eight-by-ten-inch view cameras. The sanatorium is in the background.

HEADQUARTERS BUILDING, LOWRY FIELD, COLORADO

World's Greatest
Photography School

Technical training offered at Lowry Field qualifies student for career in photography. Courses rated so excellent that college credits are given upon graduation from school.

IF ALL of the countless training courses, offered the men of our peacetime Services, embracing every Service and civilian trade, are as strong in facilities, as comprehensive in scope, and as progressive in instruction as the photography course given at the U. S. Air Force's Photography School at Lowry Field in Colorado, then indeed, the Army today offers the finest technical training available. For the photography student at Lowry studies in the world's largest photography school, a fully equipped, three-story modern brick structure built at a cost of nearly $800,000 and housing nearly half-a-million dollars worth of equipment.

With the cooperation of the U. S. Air Force, editors of U. S. CAMERA recently visited this amazing school outside Denver, Colorado. After spending four days surveying its facilities, studying its program and questioning its students, they came away firmly convinced that the USAF's Air Training Command offers the young student of photography an unmatchable opportunity to prepare for a career with a camera, whether he wishes to pursue it in civilian life or plans to stay in the Service.

As with other phases of the war-accelerated educational program of the Air Training Command, the training of photographers was virtually halted in its tracks two years ago when mass demobilization stripped the machine of key instructors and administrative personnel. But now it is back in full scale operation with facilities and instruction superior than ever. Training syllabi have been streamlined and brought up to date, facilities have been enlarged and improved and instructor staffs have been entirely rebuilt with heavy emphasis on combat experience and subject know-how.

The most revolutionary change in this streamlining program took place last month when a new course (Course No. 15201, Photographer), representing a consolidation of the Camera Technician, Photographic Lab Technician and the old Basic Photography Course, was initiated. This is a 30-week course now schooling 30 students per month, taught by approximately 75 instructors the majority of whom are enlisted men.

A look at the outline of the subjects covered in this new course provides a clear picture of the all-embracing nature of the training. (*Cont'd.*)

by Ed Hannigan and Tom Johnston

STUDENTS study and work from planes (in background) with all the latest types of aerial cameras.

THIS THREE-STORY BUILDING built at a cost of nearly $800,000 and housing $500,000 worth of equipment is the home of the Department of Photography, U.S. Air Force's Air Training Command, Lowry Field.

A 1938 Lowry Field press release provided the information for this Denver newspaper story about the first photographic class graduation.

Lowry photographic training initially had to be conducted in primitive classrooms, such as this one in the attic of the old Phipps Sanatorium (Building 254).

The Lowry photography lab and post exchange, shown at center, were initially positioned near the airport beacon tower and Sixth Avenue gate.

Activity in a Lowry photographic laboratory/classroom is depicted in this 1942 scene.

During World War II, Building 383 (center) was constructed to house the photography training facilities. Note the aircraft parked on nearby ramps and the wooden two-story barracks buildings at the top of the photograph. The three-story building in the foreground and one-story buildings to the right housed armament training.

On a winter day in 1941, M.Sgt. Louis Hechter was photographed with camera in hand at Lowry Field.

This 1942 composite image shows photography instructors and students in a variety of activities.

Foreign students were always in training at Lowry. This photograph shows Filipino photography students in a C-47 aircraft.

Another key training element that was moved to Lowry was aircraft armament. The first armament students arrived on February 12, 1938, and at the school's peak, 15,000 men were being trained annually at Lowry and at Buckley Field, a Lowry auxiliary field to the east. Lowry men in this photograph work on a Martin upper gun turret. The first armament training graduation occurred on March 19, 1938.

3705 AB. 5 FEB. '45, 183, LOADING OF AMMUNITION IN EMERSON TURRET   (RESTRICTED)

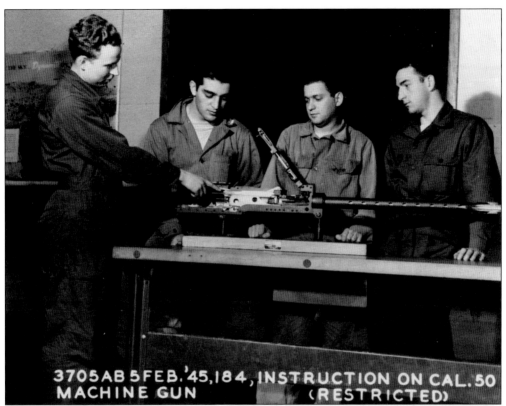

These armament students are receiving instruction on the .50-caliber machine gun.

Two Lowry armament instructors, preparing for a class, check an aircraft machine gun mount.

Shown here are the original 15 Lowry instructors. They were charged with teaching flying cadets undergoing bombardier training, which began on July 16, 1940.

Students are shown loading practice bombs, composed of 95 pounds of sand and 5 pounds of powder, at Lowry.

Three

LOWRY AIR OPERATIONS
1938–1966

Lowry Air Force Base was established as an Air Force technical training center, and it remained so until its deactivation. Nevertheless, it also served as an important base for varied flight operations for many years. In 1924, the first Denver-area military flying actually occurred at the Colorado National Guard's Lowry Field, located at Thirty-eighth Avenue and Dahlia Street northeast of Denver. This was the home of the 120th Observation Squadron until 1938, when the field was deactivated. Flying activities then moved farther southeast to the new National Guard hangar at Denver's Municipal Airport, which would eventually become Stapleton International Airport.

The Army Air Corps assigned aircraft to the new technical school location in 1938. In April, the first unpaved runway became operational, and on June 30, air crews ferried nine planes to the new Lowry Field, including the twin-engine Douglas B-18A, the new medium bomber. A four-year, $3.5-million construction program, announced in June 1938, led to the building of Hangar No. 1 and the 8,000-foot north-south runway. These projects were finished in August and December 1939, respectively. Lowry's commanding officer, Col. Jacob H. Rudolph, landed the first aircraft, a B-18A, on the new concrete runway and taxied to Hangar No. 1 on December 13. All aircraft moved to Lowry from the municipal airport. In 1940 and 1941, an 8,084-foot east-west concrete runway and an 8,300-foot northeast-southwest runway were added. In addition, Hangar No. 2 became ready in December 1940. In January 1940, there were 27 planes at the field.

From July 1940 to March 1941, three classes of cadets trained on B-18As of the 36th and 37th Bombardment Squadrons, temporarily assigned to Lowry. These men became the core group of some 15,000 bombardiers trained during World War II. During the war, Lowry's hangars and flight line were often filled with B-17s, B-24s, B-25s, and B-26s, some undergoing modification and maintenance. By March 1945, there were 104 aircraft assigned to the base, including 72 B-24s. The first B-29 arrived on May 18, 1945.

In the postwar years, due to increasing air traffic at neighboring Stapleton, safety concerns (there had been some crashes), economic considerations, and runway operational requirements, Lowry ceased hosting transient jet traffic on June 1, 1960, and assigned flying activities to Buckley Field. On June 30, 1966, Lowry Air Force Base flying operations ended. Maj. Gen. Charles H. Anderson, center commander, flew the last aircraft, a T-29, to Buckley.

Aircraft assigned to support Lowry training were first located at Denver Municipal Airport, where they shared a hangar with the Colorado National Guard. The initial aircraft included the B-6, A-17, and P-35. Lowry received its first Douglas B-18A, the new medium bomber, on June 30, 1938, while flying was still done out of Denver Municipal. An unpaved runway became operational at Lowry on April 4, 1938, but it was not until December 13, 1939, when Col. Jacob H. Rudolph landed the first aircraft, a B-18A, on the new 8,000-foot north-south runway and taxied to Hangar No. 1, that full flying operations were inaugurated.

Lowry B-18 aircraft are shown in flight, with Colorado's front-range mountains in the background.

The Lowry B-18s were used for aerial photography training and bombing practice. Lowry bombardier cadets are seen here in 1940, with B-18 Bolos parked in the background.

A Lowry B-18 bomber is refueled before another training mission.

The early Lowry flight line, with a B-18 near Hangar No. 2, is shown here as base construction continued.

Some B-18 bombers, in foreground, are in flight with various other aircraft southwest of Denver.

This Boeing B-17 bomber is one of the initial 13 that were manufactured. It is shown landing at Denver Municipal Airport in January 1938.

During the World War II years, B-17 bombers were usually on the Lowry flight line.

A B-17 Flying Fortress sits on a Lowry apron during the war years.

RND WK
SDP 9 MAY 45 47 B-17 ON THE HANGAR LINE, LOWRY FIELD, COLO

A B-17, with turret missing, awaits armament trainees near a Lowry hangar.

Another World War II aircraft, the B-24 Liberator, was assigned to Lowry when the 446th Bomb Group (H) was ordered there for training in early June 1943. The B-24 supported the intense program of training in bombing, navigation, and aerial gunnery.

The Lowry flight line hummed with 446th Bomb Group ground crew training to load bombs on the B-24s. The unit left Lowry in October 1943 and then, based in England, flew strategic bombing missions for the 8th Air Force over Germany until April 25, 1945.

The bustling World War II air operations at Lowry resulted in some notable air crashes. The memory of these incidents led to concern as residential development closed in on the base after the war. This factor became an important one in the eventual ending of air operations at Lowry.

Several crewmembers consult flight routes before a Lowry aerial photography class mission. A B-25 photography reconnaissance aircraft is in the background.

Another aircraft frequently occupying the Lowry flight line was the B-25 "Billy Mitchell" bomber, shown here on the Lowry apron.

Crewmembers check maps in preparation for a Lowry training mission with a modified B-25 (F-10) behind them. The aircraft nose was converted for aerial photography.

A B-25 undergoes preflight inspection in a typical flight line scene at Lowry.

Msgt C.R.McBride,Instructor (left) with
students in RC 47 aircraft. 1952

In the postwar years, flying operations continued. This 1952 photograph shows an instructor, M.Sgt. C.R. McBride (left), with photography students in a Lowry RC-47 aircraft.

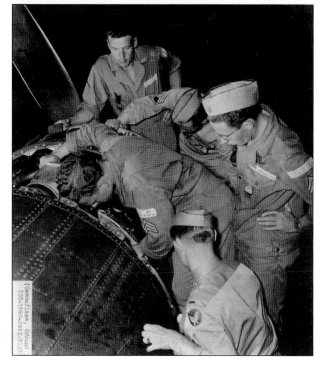

During World War II, Lowry Air Corps sergeants perform maintenance to keep the aircraft flying.

An Army Air Corps lieutenant (right) supervises maintenance at Lowry in the World War II years.

The first B-29, the longer-range successor to World War II's B-17, arrived at Lowry on May 18, 1945.

Lowry men in cold-weather clothing conduct top-turret training on a B-29 aircraft.

B-29s line a taxiway at Lowry. Note the two Lowry hangars in the background.

This B-29, photographed at Lowry on June 2, 1945, had 20 missions over the Himalayas from India to China and 17 bombing missions, with four Japanese aircraft shot down.

B-29s from Lowry are shown in flight over Denver. After World War II, B-29s simulated a bombing mission on the nearby city of Longmont, dropping leaflets instead of bombs at low altitude.

B-29s fly in formation over Lowry. Other B-29s can be seen on taxiways.

This aerial photograph, apparently taken during a World War II–era open house, clearly shows Lowry Field development at the time. The Building 349 barracks and the two hangars dominate the scene.

Due to increasing air traffic at Denver's Municipal Airport and later Stapleton International Airport (foreground) and concern about crashes into surrounding residential areas, Lowry flying activities were moved to Buckley Field and, then, on June 30, 1966, were ended at Lowry.

Four

THE WORLD AT WAR
1941–1945

On December 12, 1941, five days after the Japanese attack on Pearl Harbor, Lowry Field conducted an all-personnel exercise for air defense and terrorist infiltration. The base began to meet the challenges of war. One response was a significant increase in base manpower, both civilian and military, and in students and staff, eventually reaching in excess of 20,000 persons. Training production rose to 55,000 servicemen and servicewomen annually.

Lowry Field became part of the Army Air Forces Technical Training Command in March 1942. New facilities were needed for classrooms and housing. As a result, construction of Lowry 2 commenced on the northeast part of the base. This phase involved a chapel, theater, mess hall, living quarters (barracks), and a service club.

The training command adopted a seven-day-a-week schedule, with three shifts daily. Classes intensified in aerial photography, aircraft armament, and bomb operations and maintenance. Photography students increased in 1942 from 203 to 2,487. The Women's Army Auxiliary Corps (later the Women's Army Corps) sent its first group to Lowry in 1943 to study photography. In addition to training US servicemen and servicewomen, Lowry trained personnel from many allied countries, including Great Britain, France, and China. A highlight in 1943 was the visit of President Roosevelt.

In June 1943, Lowry opened Camp Bizerte on the bombing range to the southeast. When it closed in October, 20,000 men had received field training there.

When the war ended in 1945, the armed forces began to demobilize, and Lowry gradually returned to a peacetime training schedule, briefly serving as a personnel separation center.

The National Security Act of July 26, 1947, established the Department of Defense, which would include a separate Department of the Air Force. Stuart Symington became the first secretary of the Air Force. Lowry Field became Lowry Air Force Base on June 13, 1948.

During the winter of 1948–1949, Lowry personnel faced a new enemy: Mother Nature. Starting in December, there were 18 snowstorms in 27 days, and temperatures dropped to 40 below zero. The Lowry 2151st Air Rescue Unit, using C-47s, C-82s, L-5s, and H-5s, dropped food, medical supplies, and snow equipment to isolated towns, stranded trains, and starving livestock. In what was termed Operation Hayride (also known as Operation Haylift and Operation Snowbound), covering an area stretching from Nebraska to Utah, Lowry personnel and planes responded to President Truman's declaration of a national emergency.

Newly arrived students undergo orientation in Hangar No. 1 in 1939.

This August 25, 1939, photograph shows the Lowry "Tent City." Army Air Corps men were forced to huddle around potbellied stoves and sleep on metal beds as wind whistled through their makeshift quarters. In January 1940, Lowry housed 44 officers and 1,350 enlisted men, including 600 students in Tent City.

48

Rapid mobilization during World War II resulted in crowded troop housing. In response, these Lowry eight-man barracks buildings were constructed. This photograph was taken on September 16, 1941.

A 1941 photograph shows the interior of an eight-man barracks.

Lowry assumed an important role in the defense buildup prior to World War II as aviation cadets came to train as bombardier instructors. Between July 1940 and March 1941, cadets trained on B-18s, as pictured here. The course lasted 16 weeks, and the second lieutenant graduates became the core group that trained 15,000 bombardiers during the war.

Members of a Lowry bombardier class march in winter overcoats to a classroom in 1940. These men formed an important cadre of bombardier instructors for the Army Air Forces in World War II.

Students are shown simulating B-18 nose bombsights during bombardier training.

Lowry students learn adjustment of the Sperry bombsight.

An Army
Air Corps
master sergeant
discusses a bomb
with a pilot
and crewmembers.

A Lowry lieutenant checks out some bombs prior to a practice bombing run.

To relieve the increasingly crowded conditions at Lowry, a subpost at the Denver-area Fort Logan was opened on February 1, 1941. The Department of Clerical Instruction, which began classes on March 3, and three School Squadrons (9th, 23rd, and 24th) were transferred there.

3705AB. 9 JAN. 45, 2000,   WAC TYPING CLASS

This huge brick barracks to accommodate 850 enlisted men was completed in September 1940. When Congress approved conscription in 1940, the building was urgently needed to get men out of tents. Initially called "Buckingham Palace," it became the headquarters (Building 349) in 1961 for the Lowry Technical Training Center.

During the World War II buildup, even Building 349 became crowded, as this photograph shows.

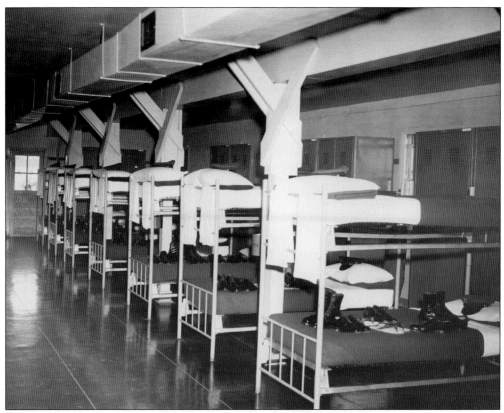

This photograph of another Lowry barracks shows a room obviously ready for a "white glove" military inspection.

A World War II Christmas celebration is captured in this photograph of a Lowry dining hall.

This "Merry Christmas and a Happy New Year" postcard was distributed in 1944. The Lowry Field insignia (lower right) appeared that year. The old Phipps Sanatorium was still featured in the center, but base development can be seen.

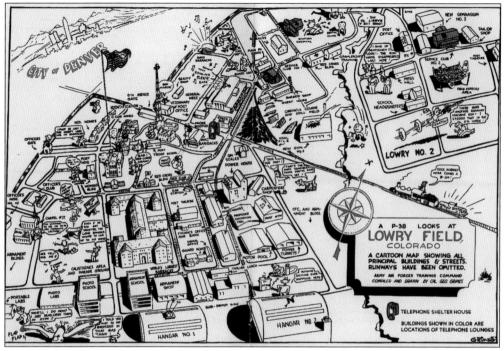

In 1944, Cpl. George Grimes produced this cartoon map of the base, labeled "A P-38 Looks at Lowry Field, Colorado."

Aircraft armorer training during World War II lasted 15 weeks. Students learned operation, repair, and maintenance of aircraft armament. Lowry began receiving power-operated gun turrets, as pictured here.

This photograph, dated May 1945, shows an airman training as a tail-gunner for a B-17.

Lowry photography training continued during World War II. Here, Army Air Corps students and their instructor pose in front of a B-25 with an array of cameras.

Photography training classes would usually have a group portrait made, in this case Class 11-42-F at Lowry Field.

Base open houses were held a number of times during World War II. This photograph depicts representative World War II aircraft. Shown are, from top to bottom, a C-46, B-26, B-25, B-17, and B-24.

Large crowds of Colorado citizens came to the base open houses to view the wartime aircraft. Note the car to the left with a sign reading "Lowry Field Salutes Air Force Day."

A fatigue-uniformed Army Air Corps staff sergeant enjoys telling some young ladies about an aircraft during a Lowry open house.

Lowry Army Air Corps personnel, likely at the field for training, relax with a game of pool at the base service club.

This 1944 photograph captures a Lowry inspection of a Women's Army Corps (WAC) barracks. The women came to the base for various training courses, then were assigned to operational units.

ICG 26AUG 44 8 MAJ.COCHRUM, LT. RAMEE, LT. WATSON CAPT. FULLER, LOWRY FLD. COLO.

On June 7, 1943, field training became a part of Lowry's program. The northwest corner of the bombing range, named Camp Bizerte, hosted this type of training. Men lived in tents for a week and worked at their jobs in field conditions. Training included instruction on chemical warfare and weapons firing.

Members of Lowry's 21st Air Service Group are inspected in field training.

(Camouflage, Ground Installation) (CO-1695-)(091-31AB)(10-14-42)

Members of Lowry's 21st Air Service Group, an integral part of America's

A trainee uses a field phone at Camp Bizerte on the bombing range. From June 7, 1943, to October 11, 1943, about 20,000 men received field training.

As World War II progressed, training at Lowry became technically more sophisticated. At the war's height, Lowry operated on a seven-day training week, with three daily shifts. This photograph shows an air crew training panel in June 1945.

Needing to expand facilities, an area called Lowry No. 2 was constructed on the northeast section of the base. Construction began in January 1942. Because the new base was separated from the main base by the north-south runway, special transportation had to be arranged and mess halls and other services had to be built there. Lowry No. 2 is clearly visible in this photograph.

3705 AB. 7 JUNE '45, 2330, COMPLETED INSTALLATION OF TRAINING PANEL AND DYNAMOTOR INSTALLATION. L.F. COLO. (RESTRICTED)

World War II aircraft, such as this C-47 transport, were used in the winter of 1948–1949 during Operation Hayride (Haylift). The planes air-dropped relief to towns and ranches isolated due to snowstorms.

This C-82 aircraft was used to drop hay and supplies to snowbound towns, ranches, and cattle across Western states during the winter of 1948–1949 in Operation Hayride, or Haylift.

Five

THE COLD WAR
1950s–1960s

The greatly reduced post–World War II peacetime schedule at Lowry proved short-lived. In 1950, less than five years after the guns ceased firing, North Korea invaded South Korea and actual fighting began during an era often labeled the Cold War. Lowry adopted a six-day training week, with three shifts daily. Courses began in rocket propulsion, missile guidance, radio-operated fire control systems, and electronic/computer sciences, in addition to the photography and armament training. With the Korean cease-fire in 1953, however, the base returned to a less hectic schedule.

During the 1950s and 1960s, Lowry progressed to the cutting edge of air and space technology. Missiles became especially important. A Department of Guided Missiles was begun in 1952. By 1962, the department supplied the Air Force with 1,000 trained missile specialists every year.

In the 1960s, the Air Force assigned Lowry a new and different mission: to become an intercontinental ballistic missile (ICBM) base. In October 1961, workers installed a Titan I missile in a newly constructed silo at the old Lowry Bombing Range southeast of the main base. By mid-1962, the 451st Strategic Missile Wing became operational, with three missiles in place. By 1965, however, the Titan missiles, made obsolete by more advanced weapons, were removed, thus ending that brief chapter in Lowry's history. The silos remain visible at the site.

The Vietnam War led to implementation at Lowry of nuclear training, advanced missile training, electronic warfare systems, and guided bomb technology. As from its beginning, Lowry training evolved with the advances in technology.

Several events occurred in the 1950s that enriched Lowry's history. From 1953 to 1955, the base became the Summer White House of Pres. Dwight Eisenhower and Mrs. Eisenhower. Mamie Eisenhower's family, the Douds, lived in Denver. While the president was in residence on the base, many national and international personalities visited. A national press corps and a 180-member Air Security Police cadre reported on and supported the Summer White House. Also, from 1955 to 1958, Lowry served as the temporary location for the newly authorized Air Force Academy (covered in detail in chapter six). In addition, Hollywood arrived when a portion of the 1954 movie *The Glenn Miller Story*, starring Jimmy Stewart, was filmed at Lowry. Base personnel cheerfully served as extras.

This photograph, with Building 349 in the center, depicts the development of Lowry Air Force Base at the beginning of the 1950s, during the Cold War. Lowry's technical instruction began to include courses in rockets, missiles, and nuclear ordnance and eventually an actual Titan ICBM site.

These images tell a personal story as well as illustrating life at Lowry. An airman stationed at Lowry in the 1960s sent these photographs home to his family with the following notations on the backs, from lower left counterclockwise: "This is the Main Gate to Lowry. This won't be the gate you will use, though, because my barracks is on the other side of the base;" "This picture was taken looking from my bed to the other end of the barracks. Cans hanging from the posts are butt cans for cigarettes;" an unidentified building on base; "This is my cube, at one of the few times it's in good shape. Usually it's not quite as clean;" "Would you believe, the roofs of two hangers [sic] The one in back has a B-52 in it;" "We were thinking of going fishing;" "This is another hanger [sic] right next to the other hanger [sic]. In it is a supersonic fighter jet used for training."

The nation focused attention on Lowry from 1953 to 1955 as Pres. Dwight D. Eisenhower established a Summer White House on the base while he and Mamie Eisenhower vacationed in Colorado. Ike arrived on August 8, 1953, debarking from the presidential aircraft *Columbine*. Here, he inspects airmen with Col. K.A. Cavenaugh.

At the August 8, 1953, arrival of the president, Mamie Eisenhower was presented with roses. Pictured here are, from left to right, Mayor Tom Campbell of Denver, Mrs. Aksel Nielson, Aksel Nielson, Mamie Eisenhower, Mrs. John T. Sprague, Mrs. Dan Thornton, and Colorado governor Dan Thornton.

President and Mrs. Eisenhower stand behind a bank of microphones before addressing a huge crowd at their first base greeting.

During the August 1953 Lowry arrival ceremony, President Eisenhower and Colonel Cavenaugh receive a snappy salute near the hangars.

President Eisenhower, accompanied by an unidentified aide, enters the Lowry headquarters Building 256.

President Eisenhower, with Secretary of State John Foster Dulles (right), gets a briefing on the post-armistice Korean situation at the Summer White House in 1953. Also in the photograph are Assistant Secretary of State for Far Eastern Affairs Walter S. Robertson (far left) and United Nations ambassador Henry Cabot Lodge.

The Eisenhowers were photographed leaving Lowry's Chapel No. 1 in 1954 following a Sunday worship service. Also in the front row are Interior Secretary Douglas McKay (far left) and Chaplain Victor Pennekamp. In the back row are Mrs. John T. Sprague (second from left) and Lowry commander Brig. Gen. John T. Sprague (third from left).

President and Mrs. Eisenhower returned to the Lowry Summer White House in 1954. They are shown here debarking from the *Columbine*. Again, a large crowd gathered to greet the president's arrival. Eisenhower remained at Lowry from August 21 to October 15.

This photograph provides a glimpse of the extensive Summer White House press corps on September 22, 1954. On September 12, the National Security Council met outside of Washington, DC, for the first time. The council assembled in the Williamsburg Room, later named the Eisenhower Room, at the Lowry Officers' Club.

The Summer White House press corps is busy during the coverage of President Eisenhower's visit.

President Eisenhower stayed in Colorado in 1955 from August 14 until November 11. He suffered a heart attack on September 24 and was transferred to nearby Fitzsimons Army Hospital for treatment. Fitzsimons (the large center building), seen here in 1946, served Lowry as a base hospital.

A smiling President Eisenhower waves his hat in farewell to friends and well-wishers in Denver as he enters the updated *Columbine* for the flight back to Washington in November 1955.

Hollywood stars Jimmy Stewart, June Allyson, and Frances Langford came to Lowry in 1953 to film portions of *The Glenn Miller Story*. This scene in Hangar No. 1, with Lowry personnel, was part of the Universal–International Studios production.

In Hangar No. 1, singer Frances Langford signs autographs. Jimmy Stewart, starring in the role of Glenn Miller, plays the trombone to the right of the microphone.

Jimmy Stewart, acting as Glenn Miller, directs the band in this scene on the Lowry flight line.

Actor Jimmy Stewart marches with the band during the 1953 filming at Lowry of *The Glenn Miller Story*.

On September 25, 1958, the Strategic Air Command established a missile base at Lowry's bombing range with the activation of the 703rd Strategic Missile Wing. Construction got under way on April 28, 1959.

Seen here are the domed structures for the control center for the Titan I missile complex on the Lowry bombing range.

20 April 1960 ground-breaking ceremony at Lowry AFB for the 703rd Strategic Missile Wing's one-million dollar missile building complex. Col Ladson G. Eskridge Jr., Lowry AFB Deputy Commander (right) looks on as Col John P. Proctor, 703rd SMW Commander (center) and Lt Col

A ground-breaking ceremony occurred at Lowry on April 20, 1960, for the 703rd Strategic Missile Wing's $1-million missile complex. Col. Ladson G. Eskridge Jr., Lowry AFB deputy commander (right), looks on as Col. John P. Proctor, 703rd commander (center) and Lt. Col. Leonard D. Parsons Jr., chief of the Ballistic Missile Division, scoop dirt.

A Titan I intercontinental ballistic missile is shown in the second stage of installation at the missile site on the Lowry bombing range.

Lowry's first Air Force Titan I missile unit became operational in April 1962. A year earlier, the 703rd Strategic Missile Wing had been redesignated as the 451st Strategic Missile Wing.

A lieutenant general's Buick staff car is parked in front of Lowry's duplex officers' quarters on Meyers Street in the late 1950s.

Six

THE AIR FORCE ACADEMY AT LOWRY
1955–1958

On July 11, 1955, a new and exciting chapter in the Lowry story began. On that day, 306 eager young men (women would not become cadets until June 1976) became the first class of cadets (class of 1959) of the US Air Force Academy. Although the permanent site in Colorado Springs had been selected, facilities had yet to be constructed. The Air Force chose Lowry to serve as the temporary location for the academy from 1955 to 1958.

The idea of an "Aeronautical Academy" comparable to West Point and Annapolis was initially suggested as far back as 1918 by Gen. Billy Mitchell. After the Air Force became an independent service in 1947, renewed interest culminated in the passing of Public Law 325 in 1954 authorizing an academy.

The Air Force Academy occupied the area known as Lowry 2, bounded by Sixth Avenue and Boston Street, in the northeast corner of the base. Cadets were housed in converted World War II barracks. Officers from all branches came to serve as upperclassmen.

Lt. Gen. Hubert R. Harmon, a longtime advocate of an Air Force academy, served as the first superintendent. Future classes (1960, 1961, and 1962) continued to arrive. The Air Force transferred intelligence, comptroller, and transportation training programs to Sheppard Air Force Base to make room for the cadets. Lowry personnel eagerly supported the cadets along with the 7625th Operations Squadron (USAFA), designated as the support unit.

While at Lowry, the academy chose the falcon as its mascot, joining the Army mule and the Navy billy goat, and established many other proud traditions. In August 1958, Lowry bade farewell to the cadet wing as it moved to its new permanent quarters in Colorado Springs. Eventually, more than a dozen cadets of the class of 1959 attained the rank of general.

Lt. Gen. Hubert R. Harmon, seated and backed by staff officers, signs an order at the Lowry Air Force Base interim site for the new Air Force Academy. General Harmon, a longtime advocate for an Air Force academy, became the first superintendent.

M.Sgt. John R. Bond (this book's coauthor, at far left) and M.Sgt. Patrick A. Kirby (second from left) greet cadets of the Air Force Academy's first class on July 11, 1955. Valmore A. Bourque (third from right in white suit) was the first cadet sworn in and also became the first combat casualty.

An Air Force lieutenant, acting as an upperclassman, barks orders to the first Air Force Academy cadets as they start their processing.

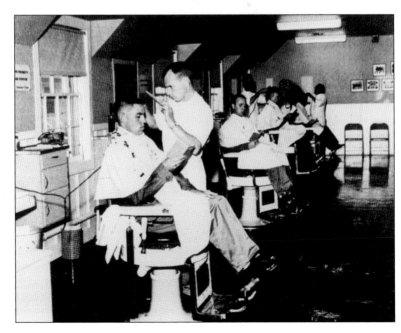

One of the first cadet processing stops was the Lowry barbershop for the typical recruit haircut, a process sometimes called "shearing the locks." A cadet studies the "Rat Bible," the cadet handbook of rules.

The Air Force Academy's first underclass was photographed with newly issued caps and uniforms. Note in the background the reconditioned Lowry World War II barracks, which became the cadets' quarters.

An Air Force officer, acting as an upperclassman, instructs an academy cadet in the proper positioning of his cap.

New Air Force Academy cadets, the class of 1959, stand at attention for the Lowry dedication ceremony on July 11, 1955. The first man on the left is Cadet James T. Carpenter.

New cadets for the Air Force Academy at its interim site at Lowry Air Force Base are sworn in at this 1955 ceremony.

Secretary of the Air Force Harold E. Talbot addresses cadets at the dedication of the new Air Force Academy at Lowry Air Force Base on July 11, 1955.

A contingent of US Military Academy (West Point) cadets, in formal dress uniforms, attended the July 11, 1955, ceremony, making a special presentation to a cadet of the new Air Force Academy.

This photograph captures a 1955 academy retreat ceremony at Lowry. Note the cadet barracks in the background.

Lowry Air Force Academy cadets stand at attention and salute as part of a typical retreat ceremony.

Air Force Academy cadets proudly march from the headquarters building (Building 905) at Lowry in 1955.

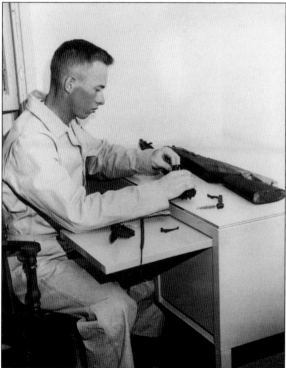

In this 1955 photograph, an unidentified cadet of the class of 1959 at Lowry wears a jumpsuit (bunny suit) as he assembles a rifle.

A class of 1959 color guard is shown in this photograph. The cadets are, from left to right, Jon D. Black, William E. Page Jr. (with the American flag), an unidentified cadet, and Arthur G. Elser.

This 1956 photograph shows the first meal of the Air Force Academy class of 1960. Some cadets are still in civilian clothes. An Air Force lieutenant acts as an upperclassman.

A newly arrived cadet gets some attention from a cadet upperclassman at an entrance to a Lowry barracks. The position of the cadet was called a "brace."

First Baseball Team 1956

The Air Force Academy at Lowry quickly began forming intercollegiate athletic teams. Shown here in May 1956 is the first baseball team.

In 1956, academy upperclassman Wayne C. Pittman pins collar insignia (called "prop and wings") on an underclassman.

The falcon became the Air Force Academy mascot. Class of 1959 cadet John Melancon shows the mascot to famed World War I ace Eddie Rickenbacker in a 1956 visit.

Buses bringing new Air Force Academy cadets to Lowry are met by academy upperclassmen and officers.

Air Force Academy cadets are seated during a Lowry Air Force Base flight line ceremony attended by parents, relatives, and friends.

The academy cadets participated in military field exercises. In this photograph, a navigation map-reading problem is the subject.

The Lowry academy cadets quickly began receiving Air Force orientation. Here, cadets inspect and receive a briefing on a Lockheed F-94C jet cockpit.

A Lowry Air Force Base academy cadet experiences an oxygen mask as part of aircraft familiarization.

Air Force Academy cadets stand at attention at the Lowry dining hall before being ordered to be seated.

The entire Air Force Academy class of 1961 was photographed in September 1957.

An Air Force Academy worship service is in progress in Chapel No. 4, Building 940, at Lowry.

The band that provided the marching music for the academy cadets at Lowry is pictured here.

In 1957, President Eisenhower attended an Air Force Academy ceremony at Lowry. Ike stands with a hat salute during the presentation of the colors.

Mamie Eisenhower, fourth from left on the sideline, accompanied the president to the 1957 ceremony and watched as some cadets, led by several Air Force lieutenants acting as air training officers, marched to the cadet dining hall.

The Air Force Academy at its interim site at Lowry was supported by many organizations. Shown here are officers and airmen of the US Air Force Academy's 7625th Operations Squadron, who provided T-29 aircraft orientation, normally used for air navigator training.

Members of the US Air Force Academy's 7625th Operations Squadron, who supported the academy at Lowry, are shown in this 1958 photograph.

This aerial view provides a glimpse of the Lowry Air Force Academy headquarters, classroom buildings, cadet barracks, athletic fields, and parade ground. City of Aurora residences can be seen in the background looking to the east.

Maj. Gen. James Briggs (right), who became the second Air Force Academy superintendent, is shown in this photograph with an unidentified civilian and Maj. Arthur J. Erickson, chief of maintenance of the 7625th Operations Squadron. General Briggs was noted for making unannounced visits to various departments and asking, "Is there anything you need?"

In August 1958, the Air Force Academy cadets departed for their permanent site just north of Colorado Springs. The cadet upperclassmen, as represented here, looked sharp as they took up quarters in their new home.

President Eisenhower addressed the Air Force Academy cadets in Mitchell Hall (the new dining hall) on Saturday, May 19, 1959. They welcomed him at their striking new Colorado Springs site. The facilities were a far cry from those at the interim Lowry Air Force Base site from 1955 to 1958.

Seven

EXPANDED
TECHNICAL TRAINING
1960s–1990s

By the 1970s, Lowry's many World War II–era wooden buildings had been replaced with more permanent structures. Five dormitories housing 1,000 personnel each, a youth center, a child-care center, a chapel, an airmen's open mess, and five buildings for the 3320th Correction and Rehabilitation Group had been added. Lowry dedicated the large Gilchrist Building to house the Air Force Accounting and Finance Center and the Air Reserve Personnel Center on September 30, 1976, establishing two new functions on the base.

Lowry's training shifted decidedly with American involvement in the Vietnam War. For example, Weapons Control Systems and Fire Control Systems instructors, who had been teaching 13 courses for the F-100D, F-101B, F-102A, F-104A, F-105D, and F-106 aircraft, began courses on the F-4C Phantom II and the F-111A bomber. Production of munitions and weapons specialists increased from 1,000 to 5,000 annually and included South Vietnamese personnel. Intelligence and supply training returned to the base from other training centers. In 1973, the North Central Association of Colleges and Secondary Schools accredited Lowry's training. By the 1980s, Lowry training began on the F-15, F-16, and B-1 advanced aircraft and on various air-launched guided missiles. In January 1980, a B-52D aircraft for armament training arrived at Lowry via ground transportation. It eventually would go on display, marking the entrance of the current museum. On October 1, 1987, the 3400th Technical Training Wing celebrated the base's 50th anniversary and noted that 33,000 students (including from the Army, Navy, and Marines) from over 300 courses graduated annually.

Despite Lowry's stellar contribution to Air Force readiness in so many specialties, a government Commission on Base Realignment and Closure recommended the base be closed in a 1991 report, citing consolidation savings, lack of active runways, and the base's high resale potential. Closure activities and transfer of training ensued, and on September 30, 1994, the American flag came down in front of Lowry headquarters Building 349, ending 57 years of training excellence.

In April 1963, Agnes Memorial Sanatorium structures were demolished, and Lowry lost a link with its past. This photograph of patient rooms highlights the open-room concept of treating tuberculosis at the time of the sanatorium's operation.

During the 1970s, new Lowry construction included 1,000-person dormitories, as shown in this photograph of Building No. 700.

Bldg 353, Lowry #1
Masonry Construction
Theatre #1

Included in new construction was a large base theater, Building No. 353.

This photograph shows the entrance to the old Base Exchange, well known to many personnel and trainees.

Construction projects in the 1980s and 1990s included this updated Base Exchange and mini–shopping center

Many Lowry students would remember the "Black Hangar," Building 1499, which housed armament training, especially that related to nuclear maintenance and electronic components.

In 1976, the US Air Force Accounting and Finance Center moved from York Street in Denver to Lowry, occupying a new, large structure called the Gilchrist Building (named for its first and third commander).

FINANCE CENTER 28FEB NO. 7

The new finance center at Lowry was furnished with old data machines.

This was a scene in the old Denver York Street Air Force Finance Center on July 24, 1951. With the move to Lowry and the Gilchrist Building, modernization would occur.

The Lowry Accounting and Finance Center evolved with a $13-million computer center to support pay records of over 500,000 Air Force members.

This composite photograph ably depicts the long-standing technical training mission of Lowry Air Force Base. Over more than 50 years, various Lowry organizational designations changed, including 3415th Technical School, USAF School of Applied Aerospace Sciences, and 3400th Technical Training Wing. Through all of the name changes, the mission remained the same: train men and women to operate and maintain Air Force aircraft and equipment.

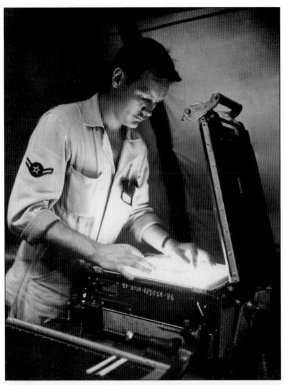

Training in photographic laboratory processing (even in the field) and photographic analysis progressed and became ever more sophisticated.

Lowry pioneered closed-circuit television instruction in 1958 and began training men and women in television production, as this studio shot indicates.

An Air Force staff sergeant trains with a handheld motion picture camera from an aircraft, a primitive technique that would soon end.

Armament training at Lowry also became more sophisticated. In this photograph, technicians receive training on adjusting a 20-millimeter gun turret.

Continuing from the 1950s, Lowry students underwent field exercises on B-29 remote-controlled electric gun turrets.

Lowry airmen prepare a remote-controlled target drone on the bombing range.

In this photograph, Lowry trainees receive instruction on a laser-guided bomb to be installed on an A-10 attack aircraft.

Lowry students in the Department of Aerospace Munitions learn maintenance of various missiles, such as this AIM-7.

This 1974 photograph depicts students learning missile guidance system maintenance for the AIM-4 air-to-air missile.

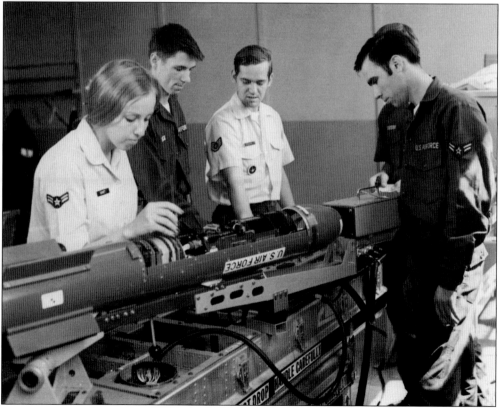

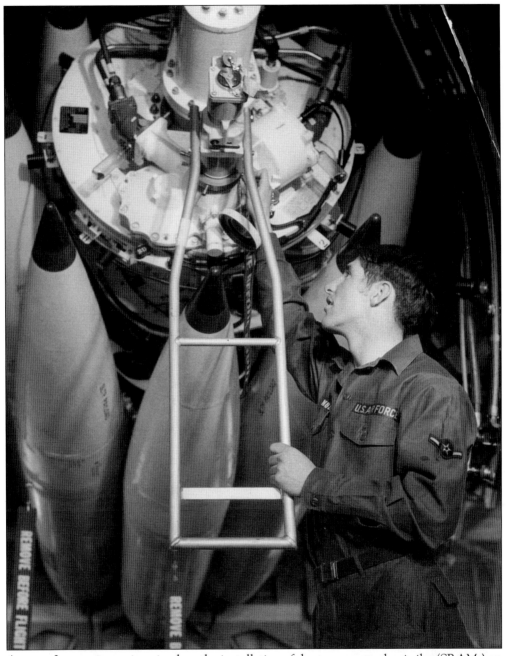

A young Lowry airman is trained on the installation of short-range attack missiles (SRAMs) on a B-52 aircraft rotary launcher.

Lowry airmen load an advanced missile pod to the underside of an Air Force bomber employed as a static trainer.

A Lowry student uses a laser gun to align the AGM-86B air-launched cruise missile to its mount.

Lowry students learn how to operate a MJ-1 munitions lift truck in the munitions driver's training program, implemented in 1974.

Electronics training at Lowry Technical Training Center (a later name for Lowry Air Force Base) assumed greater importance as aircraft and weaponry became more sophisticated. This photograph shows instruction in the High Reliability Soldering course.

Lowry electronics students often received instruction in laboratories, as shown here. The Lowry Department of Electronic Principles taught electronic fundamentals to about 6,000 trainees annually.

A Lowry student in the 1975 Inventory Management course checks shelf stock during a training exercise conducted in the course's model warehouse.

Lowry hosted training for the Department of Fire Protection and Aircraft Rescue. This photograph shows a foam sprayer in action against mock equipment.

Several types of crash fire trucks are depicted in action as students train to advance handlines toward the flames.

The Armed Forces Air Intelligence Training Center began at Lowry on July 1, 1963, largely involving classes on radar and photographic interpretation and analysis. In this photograph, Navy students receive aerial photographic interpretation instruction. As many as 56 courses were offered.

As shown in this photograph, Marine, Air Force, Navy, and Army personnel would be in training together, particularly in intelligence training.

Lowry conducted food service training beginning in 1941. A pair of Air Force instructors demonstrates food preparation with use of an overhead mirror.

As part of food service training, this student measures ingredients for meal preparation at one of Lowry's dining facilities.

In 1977, Lowry became a training center for career fields associated with space systems. In 1978, the defense satellite program moved to Lowry from Keesler Air Force Base, resulting in the formation of the 3430th Technical Training Group on October 1, 1984. This greatly expanded Lowry's satellite and space shuttle control training.

Many foreign students trained at Lowry over the decades in various career fields as part of the United States Foreign Assistance program. In 1987, Lowry trained more than 500 officers and enlisted men from 40 countries. Here, an Iranian student uses a triad student carrel, which was designed and manufactured by the Lowry Training Aids Division.

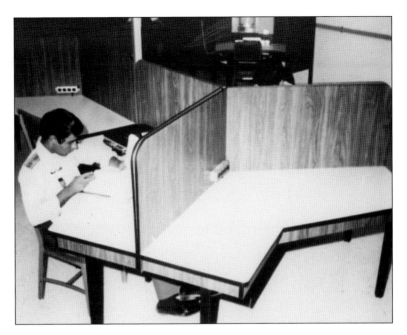

Because of its foreign student body and for other reasons, Lowry Technical Training Center hosted many international visitors. A group of Chinese officers tour training facilities in November 1986.

Lowry personnel gather at the flagpole in front of Building 349 on September 30, 1994, for a base-closing ceremony. The base had evolved from a small post of some 200 students to an Air Force technical training center that graduated 30,000 students annually. Since the 1980s, Lowry had been one of Colorado's largest employers, with about 10,000 military and civilian personnel.

The American flag came down at Lowry Air Force Base on September 30, 1994, almost 57 years to the day that Captain Stetson had raised the flag on a new air base on October 1, 1937. Over five decades, Lowry had ably exemplified the old Army Air Forces Training Command motto: *Sustineo Alas* (I Sustain the Wings).

The spirit of Lowry Air Force Base lives on today in the Wings Over the Rockies Air and Space Museum, in the former Hangar No. 1, and within the confines of the Lowry Redevelopment Authority area. Historic buildings have been preserved, as represented here by the Eisenhower Chapel. These buildings stand as a legacy of the once-bustling Air Force Training Center.

BIBLIOGRAPHY

Colorado Pride: A Commemorative History of the Colorado Air National Guard: 1923–1988. Dallas: Taylor Publishing Company, 1989.

Haulman, Daniel L. *USAF Humanitarian Airlift Operations, 1947–1994.* Washington, DC: Air Force History and Museum Program, 1998.

Hicks, Dave. *Aurora from the Beginning.* Denver: Egan Printing, 1977.

Levy, Michael H. *Pursuit of Excellence: A History of Lowry Air Force Base, 1937–1994.* Denver: Wings Over the Rockies Air and Space Museum, 1995.

Levy, Michael H. and S.Sgt. Patrick M. Scanlan. *Pursuit of Excellence: A History of Lowry Air Force Base, 1937–1987.* Lowry Technical Training Center History Office, 1988.

Lindbergh, Charles A. *We.* New York: G.P. Putnam's Sons, 1927.

Mehls, Steven F., Carol J. Drake, and James E. Fell Jr. *Aurora: Gateway to the Rockies.* Denver: Cordillera Press, Inc., 1985.

Noel, Thomas J. and Chuck Woodward. *Lowry: Military Base to New Urban Community.* Denver: Historic Denver, Inc., 2002.

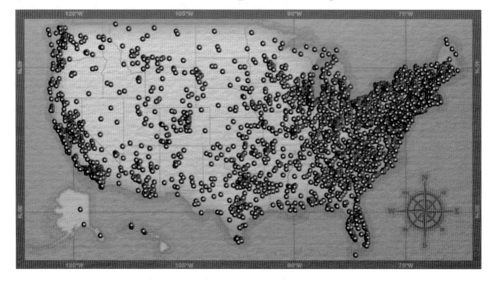